JAN − 3 2017

3 1994 01549 6588

SANTA ANA PUBLIC LIBRARY

D0438577

158.1 SHO
Shorter, Laurence
The lazy guru's guide to
    life

$16.99
- CENTRAL   31994015496588

THE LAZY GURU'S

GUIDE TO LIFE

A MINDFUL APPROACH TO ACHIEVING MORE BY DOING LESS

LAURENCE SHORTER

ILLUSTRATIONS BY MAGALI CHARRIER

hachette
BOOKS

NEW YORK   BOSTON

Copyright © 2016 by Much Shorter Ltd

Cover design by Christopher Lin
Cover illustration by Magali Charrier
Cover copyright © 2016 by Hachette Book Group, Inc.

Hachette Book Group supports the right to free expression and the value of copyright.
The purpose of copyright is to encourage writers and artists to produce the
creative works that enrich our culture.

The scanning, uploading, and distribution of this book without permission is a theft of the
author's intellectual property. If you would like permission to use material from the book
(other than for review purposes), please contact permissions@hbgusa.com.
Thank you for your support of the author's rights.

Hachette Books
Hachette Book Group
1290 Avenue of the Americas
New York, NY 10104
hachettebookgroup.com
twitter.com/hachettebooks

Originally published in hardcover and ebook in 2016 by Orion in Great Britain
First U.S. Edition: July 2016

Hachette Books is a division of Hachette Book Group, Inc.
The Hachette Books name and logo are trademarks of Hachette Book Group, Inc.

The publisher is not responsible for websites (or their content)
that are not owned by the publisher.

Library of Congress Control Number: 2016941668

ISBNs: 978-0-316-34870-6 (hardcover), 978-0-316-34868-3 (ebook)

Printed in the United States of America

RRD-C

10 9 8 7 6 5 4 3 2 1

WELCOME

THIS IS A BOOK ABOUT
ACHIEVING MORE BY DOING LESS.
IT'S A WAY OF LOOKING AT THE WORLD BACKWARD
FROM THE USUAL WAY THAT KEEPS US STRESSING
AND STRIVING.

YOUR GUIDE WILL BE THE LAZY GURU,

A PEACEFUL BEING WHO LIVES BY
A QUIET RIVER IN A SECRET CORNER OF YOUR SOUL.

By the time you finish reading it,
you will understand how to
get things done without
stress or anxiety...

How to solve your problems
in a different way.

SO SIT BACK AND LET US TAKE YOU ON A JOURNEY
INTO LAZY GURU LAND...

BEING 'LAZY'
IS A CONCEPT THAT
GOES BACK THOUSANDS OF YEARS
TO THE RELIGIONS AND
PHILOSOPHIES
OF THE FAR EAST.

IT'S WHAT THE CHINESE SAGES
CALL WU-WEI
OR...

...IT DESCRIBES AN ATTITUDE TOWARD LIFE, A WAY OF RELATING TO ALL THOSE PRESSURES + STRESSES...

A FLOW STATE

IN WHICH THE BODY IS RELAXED

AND ATTENTION IS FOCUSED.

TO BE IN FLOW IS NOT A COMPLICATED THING;
WE ARE ALL BORN WITH THE ABILITY TO LIVE CREATIVELY
AND AT EASE...

BUT SOMEWHERE ALONG THE WAY
WE LOSE IT.

THE LAZY GURU'S GUIDE TO FLOW

CHAPTER 1

PEOPLE ARE LIKE WALKING
LIGHT BULBS...

FULL OF ENERGY.

BUT THE LIGHT GETS DIMMED...

IT COMES AND GOES.

THAT'S NORMAL...

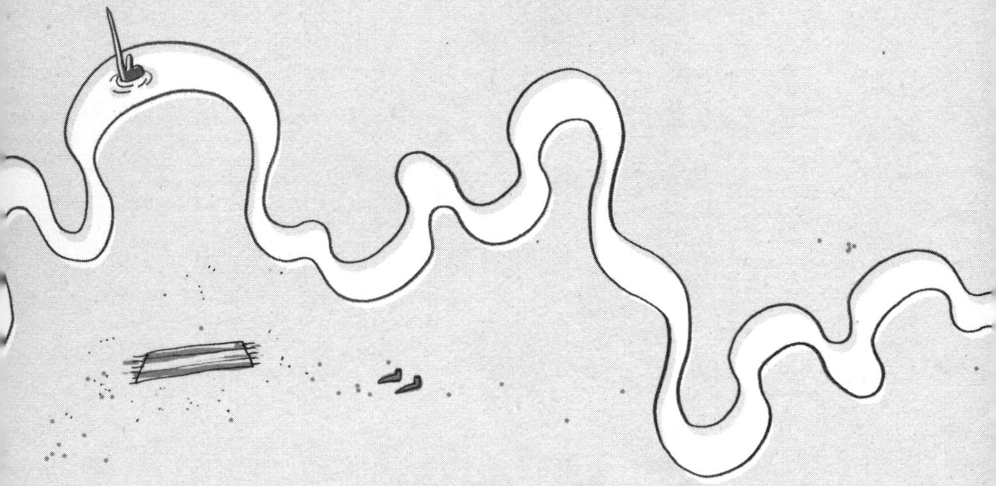

JUST LIKE A RIVER,

WE HAVE UPS + DOWNS.

THE DIFFERENCE
BETWEEN PEOPLE+RIVERS

(well, one of them)

IS THAT INSTEAD OF LETTING IT HAPPEN,
WE TRY TO CONTROL THE NATURAL FLOW.

THE NATURAL FLOW OF FEELINGS IS PRETTY SCARY.

YOU DON'T KNOW EXACTLY

WHAT WOULD HAPPEN...

ESPECIALLY WHEN
YOU
DON'T
FEEL
SO
GOOD..

SO, NATURALLY...

YOU PUT YOUR FEELINGS
INTO LITTLE BOXES

(instead of
mighty rivers)

SOMEWHERE YOU CAN

KEEP THEM SAFE

+ OUT OF SIGHT

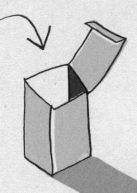

BUT WHAT HAPPENS WHEN YOU TRY

TO PUT A MIGHTY RIVER

INTO A

TINY BOX?

YOU'VE GOTTA WORK
REALLY HARD

TO KEEP IT THERE.

IT TAKES A
WHOLE LOT OF
ENERGY

TO CONTAIN
THAT FLOW

ON TOP OF WHICH...

A GAP THE WORLD IS ONLY
TOO WILLING TO FILL...

WITH EXTRA SENSATIONS

AND THE WORST PART IS...

AND WE TURN IT INTO A
NORMAL SITUATION
ENDORSED + BLESSED BY SOCIETY!

work for me give your energy

give me a salary + a car

AND TO MAKE THIS ALL WORK...

WE HAVE TO KEEP THOSE

FEELINGS

IN THEIR
PLACE.

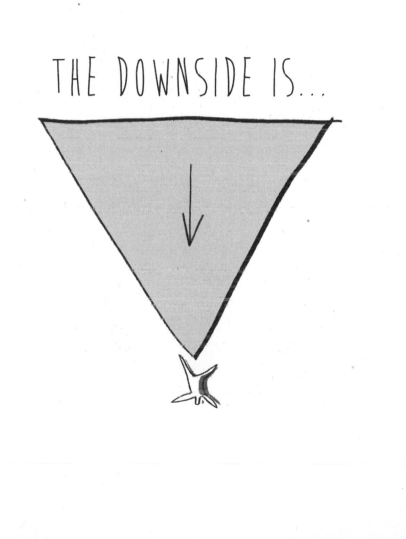

SOMETHING DOESN'T FEEL QUITE RIGHT.

IT FEELS LIKE
    THERE'S SOMETHING -MISSING-

                                    + there is...

THAT GREAT SHINING LIGHT

and that flow
of pure sensation

SO TO FIX THINGS...

WE ARRANGE FOR OURSELVES TO FEEL GOOD
SOME OTHER TIME...

WE CREATE A SPLIT BETWEEN

ME

YOU

THEN

US

THEY

HERE

THOUGHTS

FEELINGS

ONE DAY

NO WONDER WE'RE
SO STRESSED!

WE'RE ON A HAMSTER WHEEL...

AND IT ALL SEEMS SO REAL

AND SO IMPORTANT!

economic growth

guarantee our security

protect our national interest

AND THE IRONY IS...

THAT THE BEST POSSIBLE WAY
TO GET THINGS DONE...

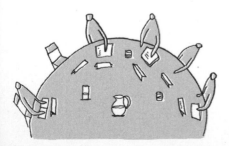

IS TO LET GO OF CONTROL...

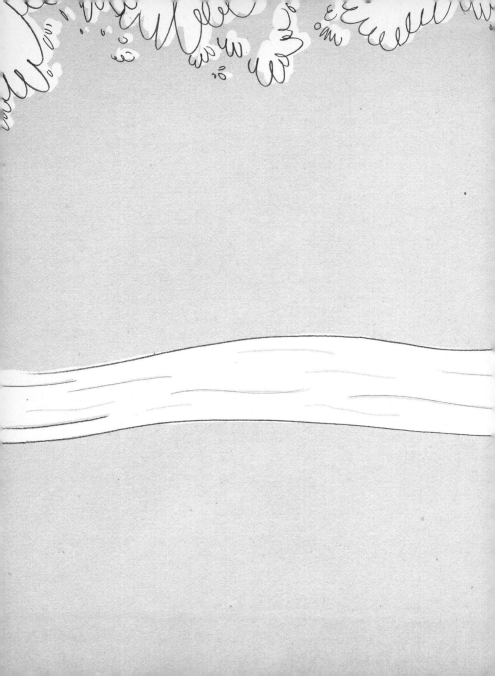

THE SELF-ORGANIZING PRINCIPLE

jam
on toast

other

1.

romance

6

c.

a.

4

work

rest.

3.

social

me-time

CHAPTER 2

molecules

tree trunk

leaves

IF WE LOOK AT NATURE
WE SEE THAT INDEPENDENTLY WORKING PARTS
CREATE COMPLEX + BEAUTIFUL WHOLES

crystals

stratos

feathers

nebulae

starlings

...WITHOUT ANYONE NEEDING TO ORGANIZE IT.

honeycomb

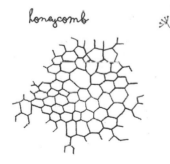

leaves and things...

WE SEE THIS PATTERN REPEATING
IN ANIMALS,
PLANTS, +
RIVER SYSTEMS

... AND EVEN IN OURSELVES!

WHETHER IT'S A FOOTBALL TEAM, A CROWD, OR
A COMPANY, WHEN PEOPLE COME TOGETHER THEY
ARE CAPABLE OF AMAZING THINGS
WITH A FEW SIMPLE RULES
WITHOUT BEING TOLD WHAT TO DO...

BECAUSE LIKE EVERYTHING IN NATURE,
EVEN OUR MINDS ARE 'SELF-ORGANIZING.'

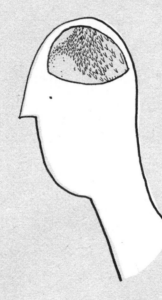

WE EFFORTLESSLY MAKE
MILLIONS OF DECISIONS EVERY DAY,

walking down the street

driving

SCRATCH
SCRATCH

scratching your head

WITHOUT THINKING ABOUT IT.

FOR EXAMPLE -

   WHEN YOU WALK THROUGH A BUSY CROWD...

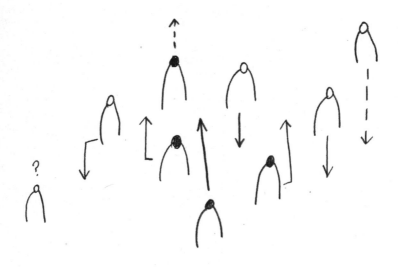

YOU DON'T WORRY ABOUT IT,
AND YOU DON'T HOLD PLANNING MEETINGS
TO ARRANGE IT.

(in fact your thinking mind
isn't involved at all.)

thinking mind

YOU'RE A GENIUS AT
GOING WITH THE FLOW!!!

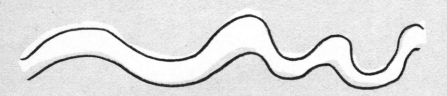

EVEN WHEN YOU HAVE TO MAKE HIGHLY COMPLEX DECISIONS

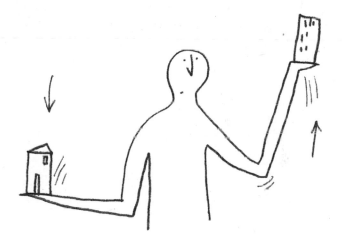

(like... where to live?)

YOU MIGHT STRESS ABOUT IT, BUT
THE FINAL MOMENT of ACTION
STILL COMES FROM THAT MYSTERIOUS

UNTHINKING PLACE.

WHY?

BECAUSE THE IMPULSE THAT LEADS TO AN ACTION
COMES NOT FROM THINKING ABOUT IT,
BUT HAPPENS ON ITS OWN FROM A MIX OF:

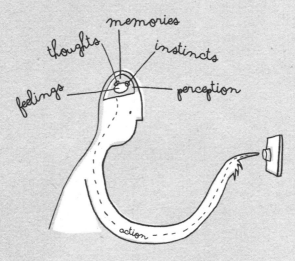

memories

thoughts

instincts

feelings

perception

action

...AND IS MUCH BIGGER THAN
THE LITTLE BUBBLE WE CALL A THOUGHT.

IN FACT, BOTH SCIENCE + EXPERIENCE
SUGGEST THAT INTELLIGENCE IS NOT LIMITED
TO OUR LITTLE PHYSICAL BRAINS
BUT IS MORE LIKE A FIELD OF AWARENESS...

... A 'FIELD' OF AWARENESS
THAT INCLUDES EVERYTHING
AROUND US...

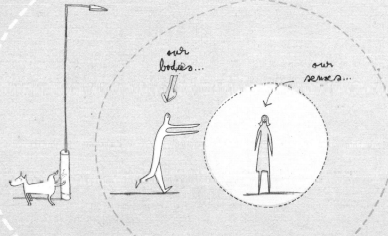

... AND THE PEOPLE + THINGS WE COME INTO CONTACT WITH.

SO WHEN WE ARE IN FLOW, IT'S BECAUSE
WE ARE RELAXED ENOUGH TO PROCESS ALL THAT
INFORMATION - WHICH IN TURN
LEADS TO MORE
CREATIVE + EFFORTLESS ACTION.

14 HZ — BETA

EXCITED, STRESSED, ANXIOUS

THIS STATE CAN EVEN BE MEASURED IN BRAINWAVE STATES THAT ARE MORE OPEN, CREATIVE, + RECEPTIVE.

8-13 HZ — ALPHA

RELAXED

SOME EXAMPLES:

A TENNIS PLAYER STOPS 'TRYING' TO
IMPROVE HIS GAME...

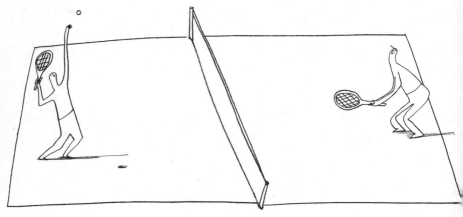

AND LEARNS INSTEAD BY PAYING TOTAL ATTENTION TO THE BALL.

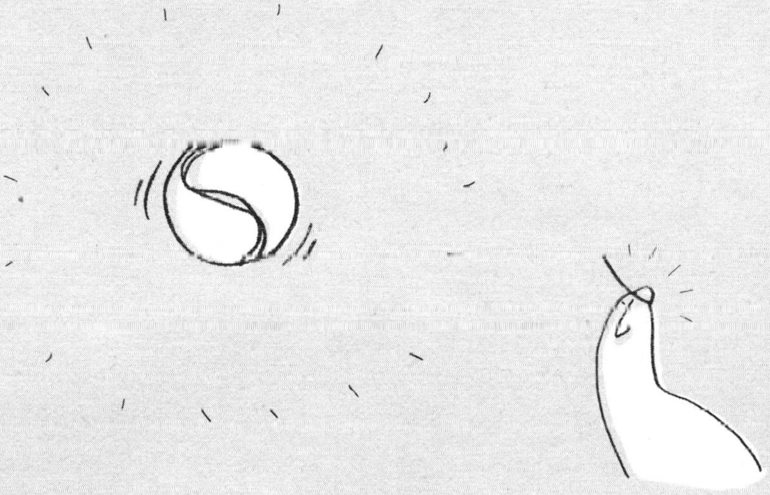

A PUBLIC SPEAKER STOPS 'TRYING' TO
THINK OF WHAT TO SAY

+BREATHES...

AND REMEMBERS TO FEEL HER FEET

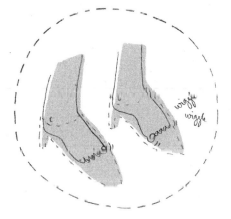

wiggle
wiggle

AND THE WORDS START TO FLOW AS IF ON THEIR OWN.

AN ENTREPRENEUR STOPS 'TRYING' TO FIX HIS SCHEDULE, DOES SOMETHING ELSE...

AND WAITS FOR THE PROBLEM TO
REARRANGE ITSELF IN HIS MIND.

MOST OF US HAVE BEEN TAUGHT THAT WE HAVE TO
WORK HARD
TO PRODUCE THESE KIND OF OUTCOMES...

BUT ACTUALLY NONE
OF THESE APPROACHES USES EFFORT,
INSTEAD, ALL OF THEM HAVE ONE THING IN COMMON...

THEY PUT ASIDE THE THINKING MIND

AND ALLOW SOMETHING ELSE TO HAPPEN.

TAKE A MOMENT TO CONSIDER ALL THE THINGS YOU'VE LEARNED
AND ACHIEVED IN YOUR LIFE.
THINK ABOUT THE MOMENTS OF INSPIRATION, SUCCESS, OR CHANGE.
MARVEL AT THE POWER OF YOUR UNCONSCIOUS MIND TO
ACHIEVE THINGS WITHOUT NEEDING TO WORRY ABOUT IT.

LEARNING HOW TO MAKE SPACE

CHAPTER 3

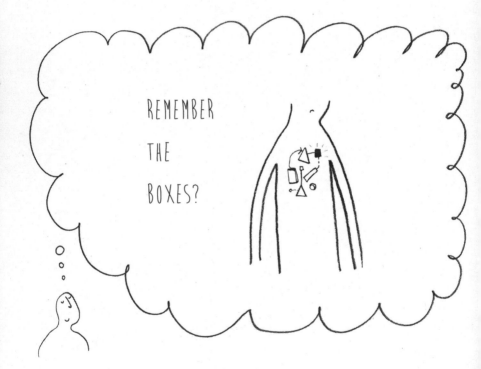

THEY CONTAIN ALL THE ENERGY
+ INFORMATION WE NEED...

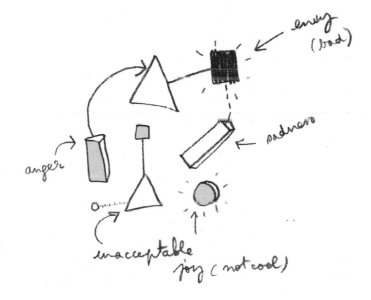

energy
(bad)

sadness

anger

inacceptable

joy (not cool)

TO GET UNSTUCK

BUT FOR SOME REASON, WE AVOID OPENING THEM MOST OF THE TIME.

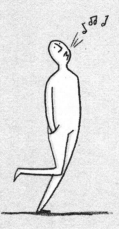

AS A RESULT, THE POSITIVE ENERGY THEY CONTAIN GETS TRAPPED ALL OVER OUR BODIES IN THE FORM OF MUSCLE TENSION, DISCOMFORT, UNHEALTHY POSTURE, SHORTNESS OF BREATH, AND RIGID LIMITING BELIEFS...

THAT'S WHY WE OFTEN FEEL STRESSED
WITHOUT UNDERSTANDING WHY...
AND CAN GET TRIGGERED SO SUDDENLY + UNEXPECTEDLY.
IT'S AS IF WE GET TAKEN OVER + FOR A WHILE
WE BECOME SOMEONE ELSE...

SOMEONE COMPLETELY DIFFERENT...

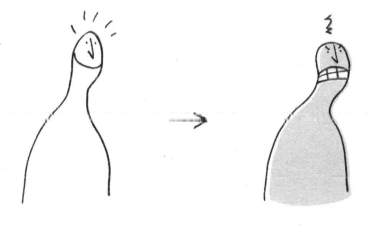

A STRESS HEAD.

OUR INNER STRESS HEAD
IS LIKE SOME ALTERNATIVE
VERSION OF OURSELVES
THAT DOESN'T LIKE ANYTHING
ABOUT WHATEVER'S GOING ON.

WHEN WE GET TRIGGERED, OUR INNER STRESS HEAD

TIES US IN KNOTS

TRYING TO FIX, MANAGE

+ CONTROL THINGS.

IT'S LIKE A SPIRAL

START HERE →

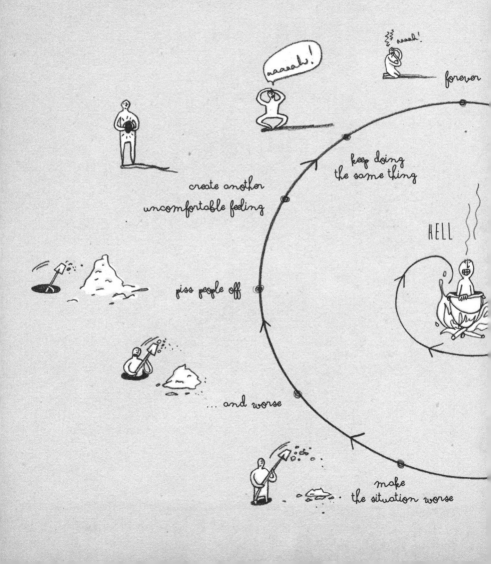

HEAVEN
all good!
danger!
something feels
uncomfortable!
aaaah!
and
ever
label it as BAD
stick it in a box and...
bad
repeat
try to ignore
the information
it's giving you
fall back on
an old response
that's stressful
because it's not appropriate
THAT LEADS US
FURTHER AND FURTHER
FROM HARMONY

... PREVENTING US FROM SEEING
OPPORTUNITIES AND SOLUTIONS
THAT ARE RIGHT IN FRONT OF US!

SO... INSTEAD OF BEING A
PERFECTLY BRILLIANT, SELF-ORGANIZING,
HUMAN RACE-SIZED STARLING SWARM

WE BECOME A SOCIETY OF SELF-PRESERVING, NEUROTIC CONTROL FREAKS

WORKING OVERTIME...

JUST TO FEEL OKAY.

SO WHAT SHOULD WE DO?

HOW DO WE RESTORE THE NATURAL FLOW

AND UNPICK THOSE KNOTS...

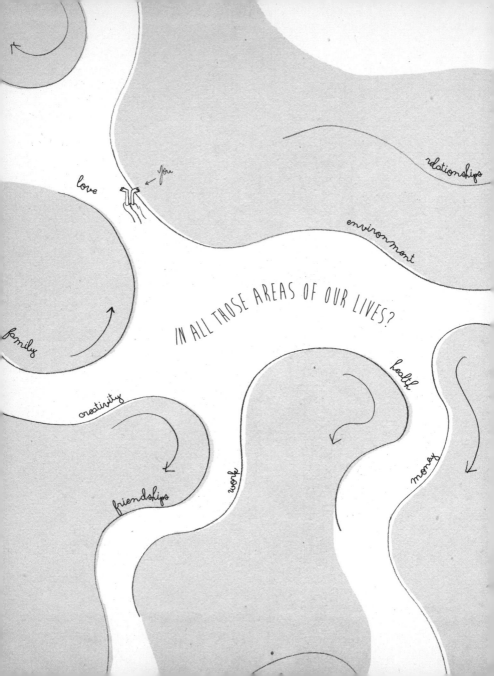

WELL,
THE ANTIDOTE IS REALLY
MIRACULOUSLY SIMPLE...

IT'S THE ART OF MAKING SPACE

FOR ALL THOSE KNOTS AND PROBLEMS

to SOLVE THEMSELVES.

MAKING SPACE...

IS SOMETHING THAT ALL OF US KNOW INSTINCTIVELY
HOW TO DO - THOUGH WE ALL HAVE DIFFERENT MEANS
OF ACHIEVING IT...

(WALKING, GOLF, YOGA, TAKING A BATH, SAILING,
SWIMMING, COMEDY, CONVERSATION)

.BUT WHEN WE LOOK CLOSELY AT THIS CREATIVE HABIT
WE FIND THAT IT ALWAYS COMES DOWN TO THREE
SIMPLE SKILLS...

THE WAY OF THE LAZY GURU

STOP

TUNE IN

LET GO

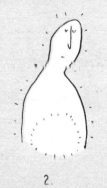

1.

2.

3.

BY STOPPING, WE INTERRUPT
THE PATTERN OF STRESS-
BASED ACTION

BY FEELING, WE OPEN OUR
PERCEPTION TO A WIDER
POOL OF DATA

BY LETTING GO, WE ALLOW
FOR A NEW ACTION TO ARISE
FROM THE INFORMATION

THESE HABITS OF MINDFULNESS RELAX THE STRESS
THAT'S BEEN RUNNING THE SHOW.

THEY LOOSEN THE KNOT INSTEAD OF TIGHTENING IT

AND THEY CAN BE DONE AT ANY TIME.

HOW TO BE LAZY

CHAPTER 4

WHETHER YOU'RE IN AN OFFICE, AN AIRPORT,
OR ON A MOUNTAIN; AT WORK OR AT PLAY;
ON VACATION OR IN BED;
THINKING, READING, OR TALKING...

1. STOP

WAIT

WHATEVER YOU'RE DOING

STOP IT...

INTERRUPT THE SPIRAL.

SWITCH OFF YOUR PHONE, LAPTOP, CAMERA, FACEBOOK, YOUTUBE... PUT AWAY BOOKS, MAGAZINES, WORK STUFF, TURN OFF MUSIC...

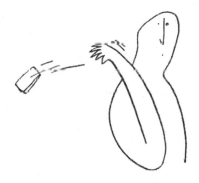

WHATEVER HAPPENS NEXT...

LET IT.

YOU'RE MAKING SPACE...

A RARE THING.

STOPPING - WHY

LEARNING HOW TO STOP IS THE FIRST STEP TO PULLING OUT OF OUR STRESS HEAD SPIRAL. EVEN IF WE BELIEVE WE ARE BEING PRODUCTIVE, WE ARE OFTEN ACTING STRESSED AND INEFFICIENT WITHOUT REALIZING IT.

STOPPING IS USEFUL FOR ALL SORTS OF SITUATIONS - NOT JUST CATASTROPHES AND CRISES, BUT DEADLINES AND DINNER PARTIES. AS YOU BECOME A FULLY FLEDGED LAZY GURU, YOU WILL BE STOPPING MANY TIMES A DAY, WHENEVER YOU FEEL YOURSELF LOSING THE FLOW. IT'S HOW WE CREATE SPACE, OPEN PERSPECTIVE, AND NOTICE HOW NARROW AND LIMITED OUR ATTITUDE HAS BECOME.

JUST STOP DOING WHAT YOU'RE DOING.

STOPPING

DISCIPLINE: REMEMBERING TO STOP

CHALLENGE: INVISIBLE STRESS

UNHELPFUL BELIEFS: 'MUST PUSH ON' 'LIFE IS A STRUGGLE'
                        'ONLY THE STRONG SURVIVE' 'WORK ISN'T
                         SUPPOSED TO BE FUN'

TIP: LEARN TO RECOGNIZE WHEN YOU'RE NOT ENJOYING
                        YOURSELF... IT MEANS YOU'RE NOT IN FLOW.

NOW, TAKE A MOMENT TO...

2. TUNE IN

SEE IF YOU CAN FIND THE FREQUENCY
FOR YOURSELF, RIGHT NOW,
THE RADIO CHANNEL FOR JUST BEING HERE.

TUNE IN TO THE SENSATIONS IN YOUR BODY.

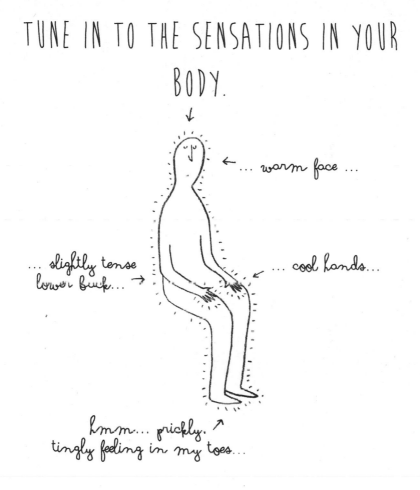

... warm face ...

... slightly tense lower back ...

... cool hands...

hmm... prickly, tingly feeling in my toes...

YOU MAY FEEL DISTRACTED, BORED, AMUSED, OR UNCOMFORTABLE.

CAN YOU OBSERVE ALL THIS WITHOUT NEEDING TO DO ANYTHING? CAN YOU FEEL THE SENSATIONS AROUND AND INSIDE YOURSELF WITHOUT NEEDING TO DESCRIBE OR LABEL THEM? CAN YOU BE WITH THEM EXACTLY AS THEY ARE?

images

AS YOU TUNE IN, NOTICE THAT THIS MOMENT INCLUDES
MUCH MORE THAN YOU ARE NORMALLY AWARE OF...

sounds

smells

FEELINGS, SENSATIONS, MEMORIES...

IF THERE IS ANY TENSION OR STRESS IN YOUR BODY,
GIVE IT SPACE, LET IT BE...

LET THE THOUGHTS AND FEELINGS FLOW.

TUNING IN - WHY

THE TIME YOU SPEND 'TUNING IN' NOW WILL BE
REPAID LATER IN ENERGY, INSPIRATION, AND PRODUCTIVITY.
BY TUNING IN YOU CREATE SPACE FOR ANY TENSION TO BE
FELT AND RELEASED, AND YOU ENGAGE YOUR BIGGER
UNCONSCIOUS MIND.

YOU ARE ACTIVATING THE SELF-ORGANIZING FORCE.
THE NATURAL INTELLIGENCE OF YOUR BODY,
YOUR MIND, AND THE WORLD AROUND YOU.

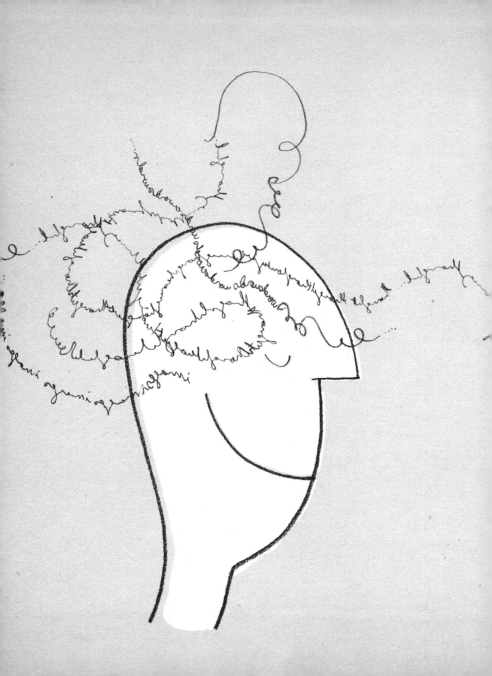

TUNING IN

DISCIPLINE: GETTING OUT OF YOUR MIND

CHALLENGE: IMPATIENCE

UNHELPFUL BELIEFS: 'I HAVE TOO MUCH TO DO' 'I SHOULD BE WORKING'
                     'TUNING IN IS SELFISH / NAVEL GAZING'

TIP: TRAIN YOUR TUNING-IN ATTENTION AS YOU WOULD ANY
                     MUSCLE. PRACTICE DESCRIBING THE SENSATIONS YOU
                     PERCEIVE INSIDE AND OUTSIDE YOURSELF IN PURELY
                     DESCRIPTIVE TERMS. BE PRECISE: TRY NOT TO LABEL
                     WHAT YOU NOTICE AS GOOD OR BAD.

NOW, WHEREVER YOU ARE, SEE IF YOU CAN...

...OF WHATEVER IT IS YOU BELIEVE
YOU SHOULD BE DOING
(OR THINKING).

NOTICE THAT THERE IS OFTEN A SUBTLE RESISTANCE TO BEING TOTALLY RELAXED, AS IF SOME PART OF YOU IS ON GUARD, AS IF YOU HAVE ALREADY DECIDED WHAT YOU NEED TO DO NEXT.

CAN YOU LET GO OF IT?

CAN YOU LET GO OF EVERYTHING,

JUST FOR A MOMENT?

See if you can relax, wait,
and open yourself to something that might
be totally unknown.

(A solution, a next step,
something you haven't thought of yet...)

Let go... Let it happen.

P.S...
IT'S NOT POSSIBLE TO FORCE YOURSELF TO LET GO.

LETTING GO IS SOMETHING A PERSON CAN ONLY DO BY GIVING UP
THEIR IDEAS AND RELAXING (INCLUDING THE IDEA OF LETTING GO).

JUST DO YOUR BEST...
NOTICE WHERE YOU ARE TENSE AND HOLDING ON, KEEP NOTICING,
AND WAIT.

LETTING GO - WHY

Letting go is both the simplest and most tricky practice
that a lazy guru can learn to master. It's as simple and as
difficult as saying 'I'm wrong' in the middle of an argument
or giving up a direction which isn't working any more.

It's not just actions we hold on to. It's also feelings -
anger, resentment, sadness, pride. these are uncomfortable
emotions but we seem strangely unwilling to just... let them go.

And yet hanging on to something - whether it's an idea,
an action or a feeling - is often the one thing that can
prevent us from getting what we need the most.

EVENTUALLY, LETTING GO WILL START
TO HAPPEN ON ITS OWN.

LETTING GO

DISCIPLINE: SURRENDER

CHALLENGE: FEELING POWERLESS

UNHELPFUL BELIEFS: 'I HAD PLANS' 'I NEED THIS'
                       'IF I DON'T DO THIS I WILL DIE'

TIP: NOTICE HOW OFTEN THE WORD 'SHOULD' CROPS UP IN
                       YOUR CONVERSATIONS WITH YOURSELF, AS IN
                       'I SHOULD BE...' OR 'HE SHOULD BE...' WHAT WOULD
                       HAPPEN IF THAT 'SHOULD' BECAME 'COULD,' AS IN
                       'WE COULD BE DOING THIS OR WE COULD DO
                       SOMETHING ELSE.' DOES IT GIVE YOU MORE OPTIONS?

SO...

THAT'S THE BASIC PRACTICE OF A LAZY GURU.
IF YOU MASTER THESE THREE HABITS,
YOU'LL HAVE EVERYTHING YOU NEED
TO START THE JOURNEY TOWARD
INSPIRATION AND HAPPINESS.

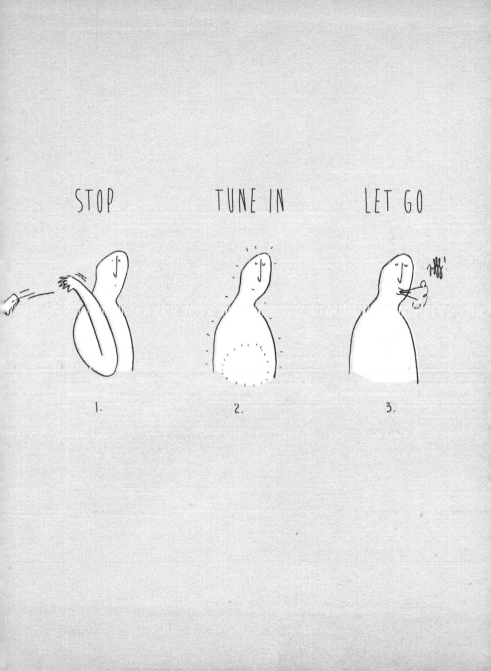

CHAPTER 5

7 PRACTICES OF A LAZY GURU

AS YOU RELAX AND PRACTICE THE SKILLS OF THE LAZY GURU,
YOU'LL START FINDING YOUR OWN WAYS OF MAKING SPACE.

IN THE MEANTIME, HERE ARE A FEW
YOU CAN TRY AT HOME...

1. BE KIND

2. BEDITATE

3. DUMP YOUR SHOULDS

4. CLEAR OUT THE CRUD

5. RELEASE TENSION

6. UNDISTRACT YOURSELF

7. COMMUNICATE

1.

THINGS GO WRONG...
MISTAKES HAPPEN...
FEELINGS ARISE...

BE KIND

THINK OF A MOMENT RECENTLY WHEN YOUR INNER STRESS HEAD
WAS MORE IN CONTROL OF YOU THAN 'YOU.'

SLOW DOWN AND REPLAY THE MOMENT IN YOUR MEMORY
FRAME BY FRAME... BE AS PRECISE AS YOU CAN.

WHAT WAS GOING THROUGH YOUR MIND?

AS YOU SLOW DOWN YOUR REACTIONS NOTICE THAT YOUR STRESS HEAD
TALKS CONSTANTLY TO YOU; LISTEN TO ITS TONE OF VOICE.
DOES IT SOUND FAMILIAR? NOTICE THAT THIS FAMILIAR
VOICE TENDS TO 'CATASTROPHIZE'
SITUATIONS - MEANING, IT EXAGGERATES THINGS...

BEYOND ALL REASON.

He keeps blinking.
I must be boring him.
I'm so boring.
    I wish I was dead.

I can't think of anything to say...
I'll never find a girlfriend.
I am such a total failure.

    Where's my mummy?

THESE STORIES ARE OFTEN VERY FAMILIAR -
LIKE OLD, OLD FRIENDS (THE KIND OF FRIENDS WHO
ALWAYS SEEM TO GIVE YOU A HARD TIME).

YET UNDERNEATH THESE CATASTROPHIZING THOUGHTS
THERE IS OFTEN A MOOD OR A FEELING IN YOUR BODY
THAT YOU MAY NOT HAVE FULLY NOTICED.

PRACTICING YOUR 'TUNING IN' SKILLS: TUNE IN TO THAT FEELING AS IF IT WERE PHYSICALLY IN YOUR BODY, A PART OF WHO YOU ARE...

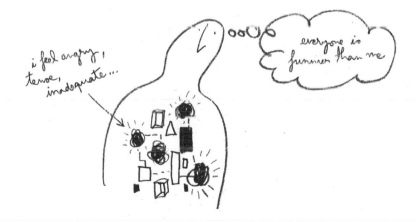

YOUR INNER STRESS HEAD WANTS TO SOLVE THIS FEELING,
TO KEEP THAT BOX FIRMLY CLOSED...
BUT YOU DON'T *HAVE* TO.

ALL YOU HAVE TO DO IS GIVE IT SPACE,

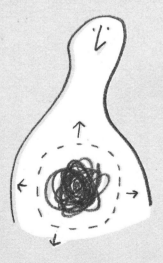

ACCEPT THE FEELING.

BE KIND

AS IF IT WERE A SLIGHTLY UNHAPPY CHILD

ALLOW THAT CHILD TO BE UNHAPPY...

JUST :BE: WITH IT

AND LITTLE BY LITTLE,
THE FEELINGS WILL CHANGE
ON THEIR OWN.

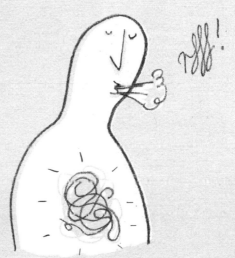

(even if ever so slightly)

2. BEDITATE

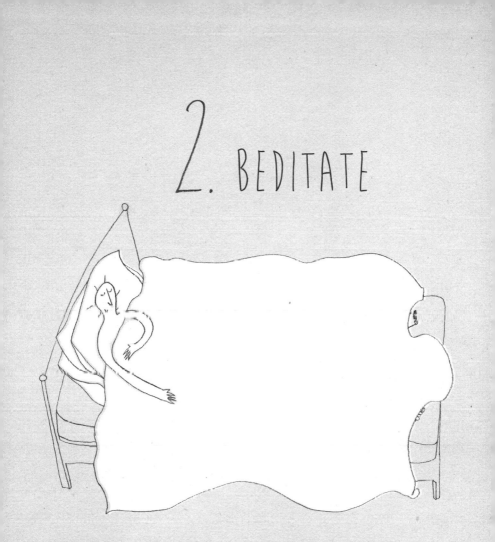

INSTEAD OF DOING YOGA, MAKING A SMOOTHIE, OR GOING FOR A RUN,
EVERY NOW + THEN JUST... DO NOTHING.

WHEN YOU WAKE UP IN THE MORNING,
FEELING SLEEPY, TIRED, STRESSED, OR ALERT...

WATCH HOW YOUR MIND GOES IMMEDIATELY INTO ACTION:
ANALYZING, COMMENTING, AND GIVING ADVICE. FACED
WITH THE TERRIFYING PROSPECT OF A NEW DAY, WITNESS
YOUR THOUGHTS LOOP INTO OLD, FAMILIAR PATTERNS,
TELLING YOU WHAT NEEDS TO BE DONE.

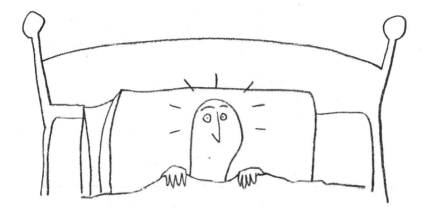

JUST STOP... WAIT...

LIE IN BED AND LET THE SOUNDS AND SENSATIONS
OF THE MORNING WASH OVER YOU...
NO HURRY, NO GOAL, NO CHAKRA BREATHING,
JUST... RELAX...
THERE IS NOTHING YOU HAVE TO DO.

IMAGINE YOUR BED IS AFLOAT
ON A RIVER

CARRYING YOU
DOWNSTREAM.

JUST BE WITH
YOURSELF.

LET YOUR MIND DRIFT OPEN.

IF YOU WAIT, A LITTLE SPARK OF INSIGHT
MAY APPEAR, PROVIDING YOU WITH ALL THE
GUIDANCE YOU NEED TO NAVIGATE YOUR DAY.

IT'S A SKILL YOU WILL DEVELOP AS YOU PRACTICE IT...

EVENTUALLY, YOU WILL LEARN TO BEDITATE
WHEREVER YOU ARE...

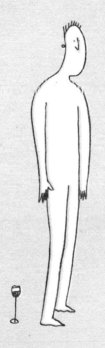

EVEN WHILE STANDING UP.

THIS PRACTICE IS BASED ON THE OBSERVATION THAT
WHEN WE FEEL UNHAPPY IN LIFE THERE'S
OFTEN A 'SHOULD' INVOLVED...
(A SECRET SHOULD, USUALLY).

'I SHOULD EXERCISE MORE '

'I SHOULD HAVE DONE THINGS DIFFERENTLY'

'HE SHOULD BE LESS OF A FOOL'

'SHE SHOULDN'T HAVE SAID THAT'

'YOU SHOULD STOP CRITICIZING ME'

'I SHOULD BE HAPPIER AT WORK'

'WE SHOULD HAVE GONE TO THE STORE'

'SHOULDS' DON'T GENERALLY HELP US TO FEEL HAPPIER LIKE THEY PRETEND TO. INSTEAD THEY TEND TO WORK THE OPPOSITE WAY.

THIS IS BECAUSE SHOULDS EXIST TO PROTECT OUR BOXES...

firmly shut

SO THEY WON'T HAVE TO GET OPENED

(THAT'S WHY THEY'RE SO CONVINCING).

YOU'LL KNOW A BELIEF IS A SHOULD IF IT
CAUSES YOU IRRITATION, FRUSTRATION, OR SADNESS;
YOU'LL ALSO KNOW IT'S A SHOULD IF YOU
REALLY, REALLY BELIEVE IT.

AS WE GO THROUGH LIFE WE COLLECT SHOULDS UNTIL
WE HAVE SEVERAL HERDS OF THEM.

THE THUNDEROUS HERD OF SHOULDS

(sometimes known as a 'belief system')

THE MORE SHOULDS WE COLLECT, THE MORE WE JUDGE OURSELVES AND OTHERS AS NOT UP TO SCRATCH, CREATING A CONSTANT PRESSURE TO TAKE ACTION.

UNSURPRISINGLY, SHOULDS CAN MAKE RELAXING DIFFICULT...

AND BEDITATING IMPOSSIBLE.

BUT THERE IS A WAY TO TAME THESE
TENACIOUS wildebeests.

THE NEXT TIME YOU GET STRESSED BY YOUR SHOULDS,

THE MOST EFFECTIVE WAY TO MAKE SPACE

FROM THE OVERWHELMING STAMPEDE

OF THEIR RIGHTEOUS OPINIONS...

IS SIMPLY TO NOTICE THEM...

(THE MOMENT THEY BECOME VISIBLE
THEY LOSE THEIR POWER).

NOTICE THE SHOULDS THAT ARE CAUSING YOU MOST STRESS at
this moment, however RIGHT or reasonable they seem...

(make sure to include shoulds for yourself
and shoulds for OTHERS).

TIP: AS WELL AS 'SHOULD' YOU CAN ALSO USE
'WANT to,' 'NEED to,' or 'MUST,' as these are also clues to
stories you hold on to about what should be DIFFERENT.

IT MIGHT HELP TO WRITE THEM DOWN...

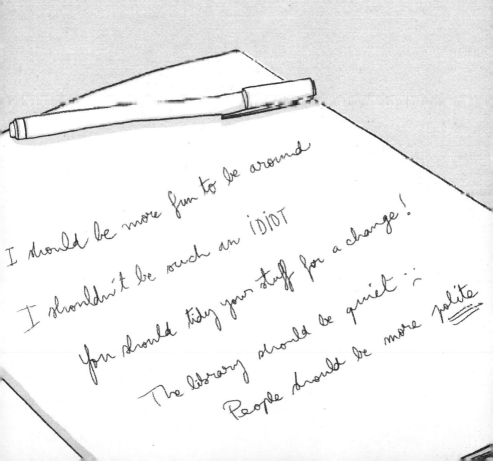

I should be more fun to be around

I shouldn't be such an IDIOT

You should tidy your stuff for a change!

The library should be quiet :-

People should be more polite

SEE IF YOU CAN FIND THE FEELING BEHIND EACH SHOULD.
BE LIKE A DETECTIVE...

TRY QUESTIONING YOURSELF:

'WHY IS IT SO IMPORTANT?'

'WHAT WOULD BE DIFFERENT IF THIS SHOULD HAPPENED?'

'HOW WOULD YOU FEEL DIFFERENTLY?'

'IS THAT REALLY TRUE?'

NOW ASK: DOES HAVING THIS PARTICULAR SHOULD MAKE ME MORE HAPPY...
OR MORE STRESSED?

YOU DON'T NEED TO DO ANYTHING WITH THIS.
JUST BY GETTING THEM OFF YOUR CHEST,
YOU'RE CLEARING A LITTLE SPACE FOR THE GENIUS OF THE
LAZY GURU TO BE HEARD
ABOVE THE CLAMOR OF THE RAMPAGING SHOULDS.

4.

CLEAR OUT THE CRUD

AS TIME GOES BY,
THE BOXES WE CREATE WITH OUR HABITS + BELIEFS
ALSO SHOW UP AS BLOCKAGES + MESS
IN OUR PHYSICAL ENVIRONMENT...

THE LOOSE ENDS ACCUMULATE,

AND SLOWLY THE MESS GETS BIGGER...

HALF OR
UNREAD BOOKS

ENDLESS
BUCKET
LIST

YOU HAVE 315 UNANSWERED
FRIEND REQUESTS
374 UNOPENED EMAILS
& NO MEMORY LEFT

... + BIGGER

ALL THIS CLUTTER
OBSTRUCTS THE FLOW
OF NATURAL INTELLIGENCE
+ INSIGHT IN OUR LIVES.

IT CONFUSES OUR INNER LAZY GURU
+ DRAINS OUR ENERGY.

SO... ONE OF THE FASTEST WAYS TO UNBLOCK
OUR PROBLEMS WITHOUT STRESS IS TO CLEAN
THAT STUFF OUT...

(PHOTOS, MUSIC, EMAILS, UNUSED APPS, TROUSERS YOU'LL NEVER WEAR...)

DELETE, THROW OUT, GIVE AWAY, REORDER, CLEAN, WASH, TIDY.

NOTICE AS YOU DO THIS HOW NEW INSIGHTS AND IDEAS POP INTO YOUR MIND — OR SOMETIMES OLD MEMORIES, IMAGES, + FEELINGS... EVEN WHILE YOU'RE CLEARING UP.

AND IT'S NOT JUST MATERIAL THINGS...
JUST LIKE DUMPING YOUR SHOULDS AND CLEANING YOUR ROOM,
THE UNHELPFUL, EXAGGERATED MOANINGS OF YOUR
INNER STRESS HEAD NEED TO BE REGULARLY CLEANSED.

ONE WAY TO DO THIS IS TO KEEP A JOURNAL...
AND EVERY DAY RECORD, WITNESS, AND SPLURGE OUT
WHATEVER CRAZINESS IS IN YOUR HEAD.

WATCH YOUR INNER STRESS HEAD...

MONDAY   TUESDAY   WEDNESDAY   THURSDAY

FRIDAY   SATURDAY   SUNDAY

LOVINGLY WITNESS ITS TANTRUMS + INSANITY.

DO THIS
WHENEVER YOU
FEEL TRIGGERED...

OR TAKE
A FEW MINUTES
EVERY DAY...

WRITE DOWN WHATEVER IRRATIONAL, PARANOID,
WORRIED THOUGHTS ARE INSIDE.

SHOW THE JOURNAL TO NO ONE - UNLESS YOU WANT TO...
(YOU NEEDN'T EVEN READ IT YOURSELF)

AND YOU'LL FEEL BETTER...

WITHOUT NEEDING TO DO ANYTHING.

5. RELEASE TENSION

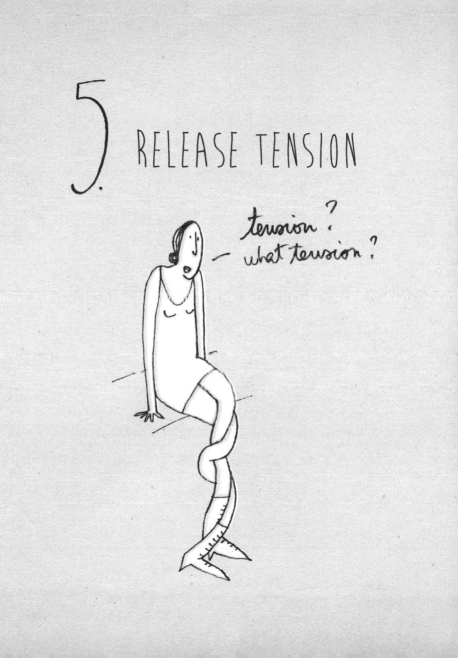

tension?
— what tension?

AS WE'VE LEARNED,
OUR INNER STRESS HEAD IS
PHYSICAL
AS WELL AS MENTAL AND EMOTIONAL...

OUR 'BOXES' LIVE IN OUR BODIES
AS TENSION AND TIGHTNESS.

THE CLASSIC WAYS OF RELEASING TENSION INVOLVE EFFORT (OR DRUGS)
TO RELAX OUR MIND AND MUSCLES...
EXERCISE, ALCOHOL, SEX, SPORTS, MUSIC
CAN ALL BE EFFECTIVE IN THE
SHORT TERM,

BUT THEY RARELY CHANGE THE SOMEWHAT TRICKY RELATIONSHIP
WE HAVE WITH OUR BOXES.

SOME TENSION STILL REMAINS...

WE FALL BACK INTO OUR USUAL PATTERNS.

A MORE EFFECTIVE WAY TO RELEASE TENSION IS TO
STOP, TUNE IN, LET GO...

AND THEN MOVE (PHYSICALLY)
ACCORDING TO HOW YOU FEEL.

ACKNOWLEDGE THE EMOTIONAL STATE THAT'S
MOST PRESENT FOR YOU NOW...
EVEN IF IT'S A FEELING
YOU DON'T LIKE

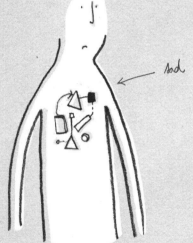

GIVE IT SPACE. MOVE YOUR BODY.

...IN A WAY THAT WILL RELEASE
+ GIVE SPACE TO THAT FEELING.

MOVE IT.

SHAKE IT.

MAKE SOME NOISE
IF YOU WANT TO...

STRETCH + FOLLOW YOUR BODY.

DO THIS EVERY DAY, FIRST THING IN THE MORNING OR
LAST THING AT NIGHT...

AND OVER TIME, YOUR BOXES
WILL FEEL MORE AT EASE
+ AT HOME.

6. UNDISTRACT YOURSELF

THE TASK OF AWAKENING YOUR LAZY GURU
IS A TRICKY ONE,

IT TAKES TIME TO UNCOVER ALL THE LAYERS...

EACH LAYER HAS ITS OWN STORY, ITS OWN 'SHOULDS,'
FEELINGS AND LIMITING BELIEFS...

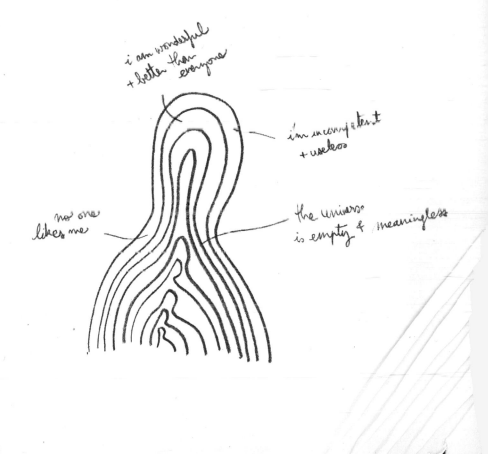

i am wonderful
+ better than
everyone

i'm incompetent
+ useless

no one
likes me

the universe
is empty & meaningless

AS YOU RELAX, THESE LAYERS WILL SURFACE AND THEN GRADUALLY FALL AWAY.

YOU'LL SEE THE PERSONAS AND MASKS THAT YOU'VE BEEN WEARING IN ORDER TO PROTECT YOURSELF, AS WELL AS THE MORE REAL YOU INSIDE.

IT MIGHT FEEL A BIT UNCOMFORTABLE...

(AT TIMES)

EVERYONE HAS THEIR OWN WAY
OF DEALING WITH THAT DISCOMFORT,

SOME LESS HEALTHY THAN OTHERS.

THESE HABITS AND ADDICTIONS KEEP US FUNCTIONING, BUT THEY ALSO CHEAT US OF THE OPPORTUNITY TO GET COMFORTABLE WITH OURSELVES (AND OUR BOXES).

THEY FILL SPACE.

SO ONE OF THESE DAYS, SEE WHAT IT FEELS
LIKE TO TRY EMPTYING SPACE INSTEAD OF
FILLING IT...

SMOKING, DRINKING, COFFEE, CHOCOLATE, SWEETS, TV, INSTANT MESSENGING,

POSTING, DOODLING, THINKING, GOSSIPING, BITCHING, COMPLAINING, SHOPPING,

OBSESSIVE GYM PRACTICE, OVERWORKING; TEXTING, SEXTING, READING, WRITING,

PICKING UP STRANGERS, POLISHING YOUR CAR, TALKING ENDLESSLY ON THE PHONE...

UNDISTRACT YOURSELF

REMOVE THE PROPS...EVEN FOR A DAY OR TWO AT A TIME:
LEAVE YOURSELF WITH NOTHING TO LEAN ON, NOTHING TO
HIDE THE CRACKS.

you with you

ONLY YOU CAN KNOW IF THESE ARE
HEALTHY + IMPORTANT PURSUITS
OR CUNNING DISTRACTIONS
FROM BEING WITH YOURSELF.

BE GENTLE... DON'T JUDGE YOURSELF
GIVE IT A TRY ... TAKE IT ONE DAY AT A TIME

AND SEE WHAT HAPPENS.

7. COMMUNICATE

STRANGELY, ONE OF THE THINGS WE FIND MOST DIFFICULT
IS TO SHARE HONESTLY HOW WE ARE FEELING WITH OTHERS.
YET THIS IS ALSO ONE OF THE MOST POWERFUL WAYS OF RESOLVING
CONFLICT AND CONNECTING WITH OUR LAZY GURU.

THIS STARTS TO MAKE SENSE WHEN YOU UNDERSTAND THE
FINAL PRINCIPLE OF LAZY GURU-NESS:
THAT EVERYONE AROUND YOU
IS AN EXACT REFLECTION
OF YOURSELF.

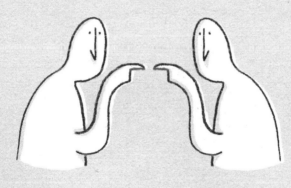

EVERYONE HAS THE SAME FEARS, INSECURITIES, AND FEELINGS -
BUT THEY SHOW UP IN DIFFERENT WAYS,
AS DIFFERENT BOXES + WITH DIFFERENT 'SHOULDS'...

USUALLY IN EXACTLY THE RIGHT WAY TO
TRIGGER YOURS!

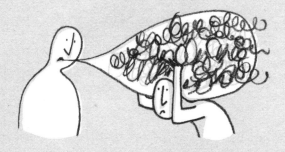

AS A RESULT,
ONE OF THE BEST WAYS TO DEAL WITH EACH OTHER'S STRESS
IS TO SHARE WHAT IS GOING ON WITH YOURS.

CAREFULLY EXPLAIN
WHAT IS HAPPENING IN YOUR INNER WORLD,
NOT BLAMING OR ACCUSING - SIMPLY DESCRIBING
YOUR EXPERIENCE STEP BY STEP.

UNLAZY

BLAMING

OFF-LOADING

DEMANDING

REACTING

TAKING PERSONALLY

DEFENDING

LAZY

SHARING
DESCRIBING
OWNING

LISTENING
WAITING
RESPONDING

THOUGH IT MIGHT FEEL SCARY AT FIRST,
THIS WILL DEFUSE TENSION AND CREATE TRUST...

IT'S NOT ALWAYS THE RIGHT THING TO DO,
BUT WHEN YOU FACE YOUR FEARS AND OPEN UP, YOU'LL BE SURPRISED
BY HOW POWERFUL IT CAN BE.

SO STOP, TUNE IN, LET GO...
AND THEN DECIDE WHETHER YOU ARE
READY TO SHARE WHAT YOU ARE
FEELING AND THINKING.

FINALLY...

WHICHEVER OF THESE PRACTICES YOU TRY,
ULTIMATELY EVERYTHING COMES DOWN TO BREATH;
IT IS THE LIVING FLOW IN OUR BODIES AND FEELINGS.

SO ANY TIME, WHETHER YOU FEEL CRAZY OR CALM...

REMEMBER TO BREATHE.

CHAPTER 6

A LAST WORD

AS YOU GET BETTER AT
GIVING YOURSELF SPACE,

YOU WILL NOTICE THAT EVERY SITUATION AND RELATIONSHIP
HAS A LIFE OF ITS OWN THAT DOESN'T NEED
YOUR WORRY OR STRESS IN ORDER TO THRIVE.

WHETHER IT'S A PROJECT, A TASK, A PARTNERSHIP, OR A CREATIVE IDEA, EVERYTHING IN THIS WORLD CONTAINS THE INFORMATION IT NEEDS TO GROW AND DEVELOP PERFECTLY ON ITS OWN.

AND THE LESS YOU TRY TO CONTROL IT...

THE BETTER IT WILL GO.

SOMETIMES IT WILL FEEL LIKE MAGIC.
SOMETIMES IT WILL TAKE MORE WORK.
BUT YOU WILL START TO FIND EVIDENCE
FOR IT EVERYWHERE...

AND YOU WILL BEGIN TO UNDERSTAND
HOW THIS WORLD COULD BE...

IF EVERYONE WAS CONNECTING WITH
THEIR INNER LAZY GURU

SO GO FORTH AND DO LESS...

AND MAY THE LAZY GURU BE WITH YOU.

THE LAZY GURU WOULD LIKE TO THANK THE FOLLOWING PEOPLE
FOR THEIR INSPIRATION AND HELP ALONG THE WAY...

CRISPIN JAMESON, MISCHA FRANKEL, LAURENCE LASSALLE, CHARLES DAVIES,
FRANKI ANDERSON, NORINA DIXON, JIM DRENNAN, JAMES HURST, GILL MORGAN,
CAROLINE WARD, JANE SASSIENIE, HADRIEN MICHELL, ODETTE MICHELL,
ROWAN DELLAL, ADAM CAROLL, SIMON CONFINO, THOMAS VAN BERKEL, ADAM
TAFFLER, MATTHEW SHORTER, CHARLIE CANNON, SOPHIE CAMU, SAMUEL VOUGA,
SIMON MYERS, DAVID BOND, GORDON WISE...

...AND THE ORIGINAL LAZY GURU, SATYANANDA.

LAURENCE SHORTER is an author, leadership consultant and stand-up comedian. In his quest to attain true happiness, he has performed a one-man show at the Edinburgh Festival, authored a bestselling book on optimism (*The Optimist: One Man's Search for the Brighter Side of Life*), and traveled the world consulting to global organizations. He currently lives in a creative community in East Sussex.

MAGALI CHARRIER is an award-winning illustrator, animator, and filmmaker. She lives in East London with her partner and son Marlow.

To stay in touch, get involved, and share inspiration for a stress-free life, please visit us at www.lazyguru.co.uk.